I0605577

read my lips

read my lips

UNDERSTANDING THE HIDDEN MESSAGES IN YOUR KISS

JILLY EDDY

STERLING ETHOS
New York

STERLING ETHOS
New York

STERLING ETHOS and the distinctive Sterling Ethos logo
are registered trademarks of Hachette Book Group, Inc.

ISBN 978-1-4549-6232-8
ISBN 978-1-4549-6233-5 (e-book)

Library of Congress Control Number: 2025937490

Sterling Ethos books may be purchased in bulk for business,
educational, or promotional use. For more information, please
contact your local bookseller or the Hachette Book Group's Special
Markets department at special.markets@hbgusa.com.

Printed in China

2 4 6 8 10 9 7 5 3 1

unionsquareandco.com

Cover design by Kaylie Pendleton
Interior design by Stacy Forte
Front cover image by Lana Brow/Shutterstock.com. Interior pattern
by Yasminepatterns/Shutterstock.com.
Back cover and interior lip images courtesy of Jilly Eddy

Dedicated to Mr. Max,
August 2019 to February 2025

contents

features of the lip print:
uncommon marks

INTRODUCTION

Eyes may be the windows into the soul, but lips are where the magic happens! They're not just for smooching the ones you love or shaping breath into words. This book is all about how to understand their physical form and how they communicate more about you—and the people around you—than you ever thought was possible. You're about to have a fun adventure. This book is a guide to understanding the hidden messages in your lip prints.

In this book you'll find easy-to-understand information regarding what the shape, size, color intensity, corners, spacing, fullness, and other markings of your lip prints have to say about you and to you. More than a hundred categories and subcategories are included here, each with examples of individual diagrams and actual lip prints.

Each section includes extraordinary anecdotes, showing how giving and receiving lip prints can open up a whole new world of interaction and intimacy, which people are craving. You'll find this process—which I developed and call Lipsology®, the art and science of lip print reading!—is fun, informative, and amazingly accurate.

Once you've read even part of this book, you'll find yourself staring at people's lips. You'll wonder what their lip prints would look like on paper (on a cheek, a napkin, a coaster, or the back of a business card), and you'll want them to put lipstick on and kiss paper for you. They'll be intrigued by what you're doing, and they'll want to kiss paper for you so you can read them like a book!

So, enjoy collecting lip prints and learning how to read them. Soon you'll be using your new lip print reading skills to communicate with others in a unique, caring, and playful way. Go ahead—use this knowledge to be the life of the party reading your friends' and family's lip prints!

getting started

This book will give you easy-to-use guidelines for interpreting each print you make. Have fun learning more about the unique features of your lip prints and the lip prints of the people around you!

Let's start with the equipment needed.

MATERIALS

- Lipstick (dark or bright colors are best, avoid "long lasting" products that dry too fast)
- Paper (white, smooth, plain, non-glossy; a small sketch pad is useful)
- Kiss Cards (optional, a specially designed paper or card for a party or event); see examples on page 128
- Pen (to jot down pertinent information)
- Mirror (optional)
- Tissue (optional)
- Magnifying glass (optional)
- Ruler (optional)
- Your lips, of course

Please keep in mind, there's no right or wrong way to make lip prints. Whatever you want to do is the right way. The messages from your lip prints are from you to you, and Lipsology is your interpreter.

Here are the steps:

- Apply lipstick.
- Make one, two, or more lip prints on the same piece of paper or Kiss Card.
- Note which lip print was first, second, etc.
- If you rotated the paper, indicate which way is up.
- Sign and print your name and the date next to your lip prints.

LIP PRINT MARKINGS AND INTERPRETATIONS

Lip print categories are organized into two groups:

- The marks that everyone has (common marks)
- The marks that may or may not be revealed in your lip prints (uncommon marks)

Focus on the first lip print you make. Use the lip print examples throughout the book to help you identify which subcategory best matches it. Then you'll be ready to read the interpretation. If you can't decide between two subcategories, read both and see which fits you best (maybe both fit you perfectly). If your other prints are similar, you're done; otherwise, repeat the process.

Your lip prints will vary, just as your kisses vary depending on who you're kissing, how you're feeling, what's going on in your life, and where you are. Because of all the factors that can influence their appearance, read your lip prints often for up-to-date information.

It's important for you to understand the significance of the upper and lower lip.

Your upper lip reflects your external world. This includes how others perceive you, how you interact with others, and how emotional and affectionate you are. Injury or trauma to a person's upper body (from the waist to the top of the head) can also be revealed here.

Your lower lip reflects your internal world. This includes your private side, feelings, sense of humor, eating preferences, health issues, and your notions of sentiment and romance. Injury or trauma to your lower body (from your waist to the bottom of your feet) can also be shown here.

It's a good idea to check all of the subcategories, because sometimes you may think a print matches a certain subcategory, then change your mind. For example, at first the shape of your lip print says you're a diamond, but later it looks round or oval. In that case, read both to learn more about what your lip prints have to say. You will find something about yourself in *all* of the following categories:

- Color Intensity
- Size
- Shape
- Fullness
- Hug Pucker
- Cupid's Bow
- Gourmet Lip Split
- Spacing
- Corners

NOTE: There are three categories with a "no" subcategory: No Hug Pucker, No Cupid's Bow and No Gourmet Lip Split. Don't miss them; they also have interesting meanings.

features of the lip print:

common marks

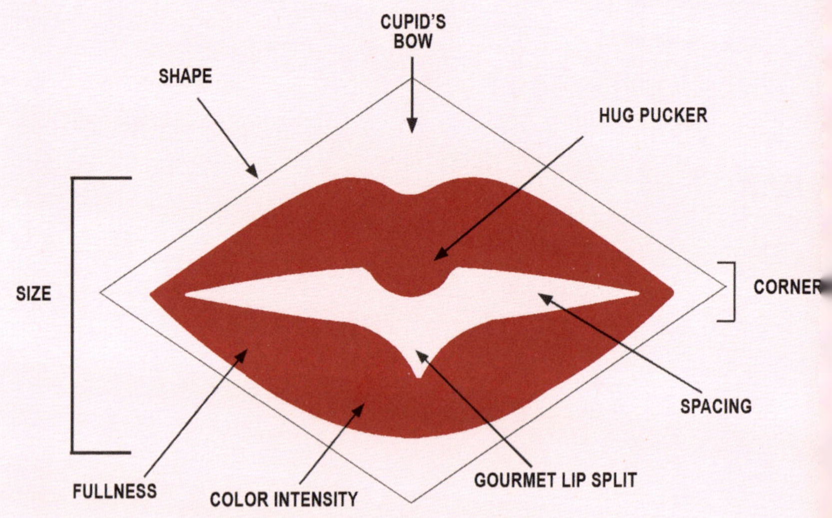

LIP MAP

common marks

Before you start making lip prints and interpreting them, it's a good idea to understand general lip print features. The Lip Map on the left contains the characteristics you will recognize on your own lip prints, or the prints of the people you are doing readings for. There are many more categories and subcategories, but these are the categories everyone has.

I know you're excited to get started, so you can, of course! Start by making just one lip print. Look at it and then compare it against the Lip Map. Pick a category—try Color Intensity and see what message your lips have for you.

You can also open randomly to a category and see if you have the mark you opened to.

If you're a person who likes to systematically study and learn each category, it's best to do so in the order presented in this little book, starting with Color Intensity, until you have mastered these common marks. Keep your copy of *Read My Lips* nearby in case you need a little help.

COLOR INTENSITY

DARK COLOR
UPPER AND
LOWER

UPPER LIP
LIGHTER THAN
LOWER

MEDIUM COLOR
UPPER AND
LOWER

UPPER LIP
DARKER THAN
LOWER

LIGHT COLOR
UPPER AND
LOWER

MOTTLED UPPER
AND LOWER

COLOR INTENSITY

Color intensity reflects your outward and reserve energy. Surprisingly, "color intensity" does not totally depend on the shade of lipstick you apply. A dark shade might produce darker or lighter lip prints, depending on other factors, such as application, pressure, and so on.

Multiple lip prints with different color intensity tell a story about how your energy changes. It's important to number each print you make because the story differs depending not only on the look of the print but also on the order each lip print is made and the location on the paper. You'll learn more about this in the section "Position of Prints on Paper" (see page 113).

DARK COLOR UPPER AND LOWER

Your outward and reserve energies are strong, making you the Cheerleader—the "rah, rah" person of the group! Taking care of yourself results in lots of energy, and others recognize it when they see you. Sometime during your life you may be the boss, the business owner, or a member of the board of directors (maybe all three).

- Once you decide what you want to do, there's no reason why you can't succeed.
- You use your joy and enthusiasm to accomplish your desires.
- You have excellent leadership qualities and are good at getting others to buy into your ideas.

The Art of Lip Coloring

Gold dip pink, baroque bronze, crimson red, Persian melon, lilac mist—lipstick colors pretty enough to paint a picture with. When you create a lip print, your canvas is any kissable surface. Your lipstick-painted lips are your brush. Apply your favorite brand and color, then press your lips to paper to reveal your kiss's hidden messages.

In the days before lipstick, the only commercially available product was red and came in a jar or pot, so you needed to apply lip color with either a brush or your fingers. Today, your lipstick probably comes in a cylinder-shaped tube with a cover, a distant relative of Maurice Levy's 1915 invention.

We owe the start of different lipstick color choices to Elizabeth Arden, who started introducing them in the early 1930s, inspiring other companies to add different shades to their lipstick palettes.

Just as any artist has different media and colors at their command, so it is with the lipstick artist, mixing and experimenting to create the desired look. You can even use a tinted lip gloss that tastes like strawberry, peppermint, peach, raspberry, vanilla . . . and it smells wonderful, too!

MEDIUM COLOR UPPER AND LOWER

Your outward and reserved energies are average because usually you know when to rest and are steadily active, productive, and reliable. But sometimes you run out of energy and/or time to accomplish everything on your to-do list.

- Balancing work, play, school, and family is important to you, and you can handle them all for a while, but not forever.
- Consider taking the time to prioritize where your energy goes; decide what is most important for you to do and put your energy there first.

LIGHT COLOR UPPER AND LOWER

Your outward energy and reserve energy are both low. I call these "Ghost Lips." Your lip prints are reflecting back to you that you need some time for yourself without concerns for anyone else's issues. Take as good care of yourself as you lovingly do for others. Also, take time to meditate, recharge your battery, and discover what it's like *not* to be exhausted.

If this describes you, gift yourself a "breathing room experience" (on an as-needed basis): a sufficient buffer of time or space for freedom of movement or relief from a given source of pressure or stress. Here are some tips:

- Go as soon as you possibly can.
- Plan to go someplace away from home.
- Aim for three days minimum.
- Leave any electronics at home. (This may be easy for you. If it's difficult, please limit your use.)

- Have no hidden agendas. Don't combine your breathing room experience with your brother's wedding, a business conference, or a shopping spree.
- Go by yourself! For some this will be easy to do, and they will love having some alone time. For others it may be very difficult. Remember, it's best to do what works for you.
- Put your lip prints on the refrigerator (as a reminder) until you go.

The idea is for you to get up, take a nap, go to bed whenever you want (no electric or battery-operated alarm). Go for a meandering walk, skip, run, do yoga or aerobics (because *you* want to). Sip a beverage and stare at your dog or gaze out the window. Don't get dressed all day! Soak in a hot tub, get a massage. Read a real book! Eat when and what you want. When you come home, you'll know what it's like to feel refreshed!

UPPER LIP LIGHTER COLOR THAN LOWER

Your outward energy is low, but your reserve energy is strong. Others have to push you to do things; you're the first one wanting to quit or go home. You never seem to have enough energy to do what someone else wants you to do. Yet, if it's your own idea and something you really want to do, you have plenty of energy.

- Your upper lip print is suggesting that if you rest more often, you may have enough energy to help others and do what they want to do.

- Keep in mind that it's great to have reserve energy to do what you want. But it's also wonderful to have enough energy to do something fun with your friends and to help others when you can.

UPPER LIP DARKER COLOR THAN LOWER

Your outward energy is strong, but your reserve energy is low. Everyone thinks you can jump, run, dance, and sing . . . that you can pretty much go on forever. And that's what you want others to think, but your lighter lower lip is warning you to take time for a rest.

- You're known for putting lots of energy into helping others, getting needed projects done, and doing fun things.
- Take care to not overdo! Remember—that includes things that you love, too.

MOTTLED UPPER AND LOWER

This is not a good sign, especially if it's more light than dark. Your outward and reserve energies fluctuate. Light color = tired; dark color = peppy. You tend to go, go, go, like the Energizer Bunny, until you crash. When others ask you to add more to your already-full plate, try to weigh "yes" versus "no" instead of immediately saying "yes," which you tend to do. Learn to say "I need to think about it" or "I'll get back to you."

- If it's not in your best interest to take on more responsibility, it's not good for the other person, either.
- Get back to the person in a timely manner.

Color Intensity Story

Once I did a reading for a young lady at a Seattle Design Center party. She was beautiful and smartly dressed, but her lip prints were all washed out and ghostly looking. She gave me her lip prints and said she hoped I could see them enough to read them, that she must not have pressed hard enough or used a dark-enough color, and that she really didn't like how they looked.

She looked great, but her lip prints told me that she was exhausted, spread thin, stressed out, and in need of a relaxing spa holiday. When I told her, she looked amazed and said I was "right on!" She went on to explain that she was raising three kids as a single parent, going to school full time, and working full time—her lip print reflected this.

SIZE

Lip size demonstrates how a person tackles projects. Part of determining the size of your lip print has to do with your intuitive perception. Pay attention to your first impression. Sometimes a lip print will seem to fit somewhere between two sizes. Both probably apply. This is also true when you have multiple lip prints that are different sizes. Both descriptions will contribute to an accurate reading.

Width includes Zingers (see page 71), Angel Wings (see page 72), and Pushing Bar (see pages 85 and 86).

LARGE

2¼" to 3" wide by 1½" to 3" high (the largest lip print in my collection is 3" by 3")

You like to do things big, and you like to do things right, with the right tools. You don't like others nitpicking about how much the project is going to cost or when you'll complete it. You're fair with others, and you expect others to be fair with you. You don't like to be rushed—you're all about quality work, not the fastest turnaround. You like to finish what you start. Seeing a project through to completion in a timely manner is important to you. (And nothing is more frustrating than someone starting a project for you and not finishing it in a timely manner.)

- You prefer to do it right or not at all. Go big or go home!
- If you can't have free rein, you usually don't want to play!

MEDIUM

1¾" to 2¼" wide by 1¼" to 2¼" high

You're a Juggler. You've mastered the ability to handle more than one project at a time. Even though time management and allocation of resources for your projects can be challenging, you amaze others at how you always land on your feet. Balance is important to you: work/play, children/work, relationships/work, or children/relationships. Whatever it is, you strive to reach a comfortable place.

- You have a tendency to beat yourself up when everything isn't going as smoothly as you'd like.
- You're doing a great job, and you should choose to focus on what's going well, take credit for your accomplishments, and ask for help when you need it.
- Don't take on any more projects at this time. Knowing when to say "no" is as important as knowing when to say "yes."

SMALL

⅞" to 1¾" wide by ⅝" to 1¼" high (the smallest lip print in my collection is ⅞" by ⅝")

You're detail-oriented, well-organized, and work hard to finish your projects on time and under budget. You like to have plenty of information before you start a new project. You're a master at work that requires attention to minute details and meticulous results. You're good with facts and figures; it's important to you that the facts and figures are accurate because your decisions are based on them.

You're an excellent project manager.

- You don't take anything for granted.
- You study the steps necessary to meet your goals.
- After careful consideration, you move ahead.

SHAPE

DIAMOND

TRIANGLE

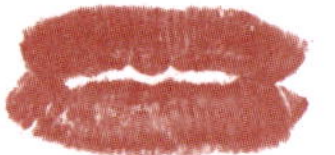

RECTANGLE/
SQUARE

ROUND/OVAL

WAVY

WAVY UPPER

WAVY LOWER

SHAPE

Shape refers to the outside perimeter of your lip print with protrusions (for example, "Pushing Bar," page 85).

Keep in mind that even though you may decide on the shape, sometimes a single print will seem to morph. For example, what looks like a diamond may suddenly look more like an oval. In this case, both may apply. Read both descriptions to get more information about the shape.

- Shape indicates how successful you are and in what ways.
- Shape also indicates how easy you are to get along with and how you deal with conflict.

DIAMOND

People with diamond-shaped lip prints sparkle and shine like the Centenary Diamond. Whatever you do, whether it's your career or home life, you do it very well. You're successful, competent, and accomplished, and receive satisfaction, sometimes emotionally or monetarily, and often both.

- You're a wonderful mentor, actively helping others achieve success.
- You give generously to the community. (And if you don't, you can start today!)
- Also note you have all the qualities of the person with triangular-shaped lip prints because it takes two triangles to make a diamond.

TRIANGLE

You're a natural Talent Scout with a unique ability to recognize talents in others. Much of what you do is behind the scenes, helping others achieve their goals and dreams.

- From a solid base, you point others in the right direction.
- Your vision and support help others overcome their challenges and learn to succeed on their own.

RECTANGLE/SQUARE

You're very well grounded in what you believe and know what you need to do. Your family and friends know you're there for them. If they need your advice, your muscle, even your money, you're their Go-to Person. You're firmly planted, not easily knocked over, like a Stonehenge vertical sarsen.

- People look to you for guidance, clarity, and direction.
- If you have this lip print shape, you're also referred to as a Godfather or Godmother because of your solid position in your family and community.
- You know who you are and what you need to do.

ROUND/OVAL

You like things to run smoothly, and often play the part of the Peacemaker. You don't like conflict, controversy, or confusion. You like to work cooperatively with others. You look out for others and are happiest when everyone else is happy, too!

- You often ask, "How can I help?"
- Sometimes you apologize, "I'm so sorry that happened, it must have been my fault," even if it isn't your fault. You want everyone to get along, make amends, and avoid hurt feelings.

NOTE: There is an unexpected contradiction: round with Zingers. These people like things to go smoothly and do not like to fight or argue. However, they have the ability to verbally nail people to the wall, or at least speak their minds when needed (see "Zingers," page 71).

WAVY

It's important to note that, unlike the other shapes, wavy lip prints have lots of curves, indentations, protrusions, and irregularities on the outer edges of your lip print. These indicate you are artistic or creative in some way. Sometimes the waviness is obvious and sometimes it's more subtle.

Wavy Lines on Both Upper and Lower

This indicates you are very artistic. You might be any kind of artist: musician, painter, sculptor, jewelry maker, gourmet cook, actor, or writer.

- You have a vivid imagination.
- You're actively using your talent and proud of your work.
- Your talent is known and appreciated by others.

Wavy Upper (but Not Lower)

Wavy lines on only the upper lip show you're creative and your work is known and enjoyed by others, but you may need praise and reassurance that you're doing a great job.

Wavy Lower (but Not Upper)

Wavy lines on your lower lip indicate you might be privately creative. You enjoy your own work, but don't share your creations with others. Wavy on lower outer edge only can also indicate hidden talent you haven't taken the time to express. You might consider tapping into this inner creativity to cultivate and express it.

NOTE: Not having wavy lip prints doesn't mean you're not creative. You may be the most artistic person in the world, but your lip prints don't show it at this reading.

Shape Story

At the Pacific Northwest Writers Association Conference, during a break, I joined a long line for the women's restroom. Several of them were talking about how I read lip prints, which I had shared during our class together, so I offered to do quick readings. The next thing I knew, I had a line of my own. I heard someone behind me say, "You should do this, too." Another voice responded, "Okay."

I grabbed the next person's lip print card, then extended my hand and said, "Congratulations!" "What for?" she said. I responded, "Because you have diamond-shaped lip prints. That tells me you're very successful, extremely competent and accomplished, and very well known for what you do."

Laughter erupted from the crowd and a few squeals of "Oh, my God!"

"Well, I don't know what's so funny, that's what her lip prints reveal," I insisted. "Also, you're a mentor and help others to become successful."

When I moved my thumb, which had been covering the lady's signature, I realized I'd been reading the lip prints of Jean M. Auel, bestselling author of the Earth's Children series, including *The Clan of the Cave Bear*, and the keynote speaker for that evening. I looked up and grinned. "Aren't I good?"

She was grinning, too. "Yes! I like this! Can I have your business card?"

FULLNESS

UPPER AND
LOWER LIP FULL

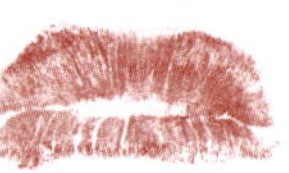

UPPER FULLER
THAN LOWER

LOWER FULLER
THAN UPPER

UPPER AND LOWER
LIP THIN

UPPER AND LOWER LIP
AVERAGE

UPPER OVERREACHES
LOWER

LOWER OVERREACHES
UPPER

FULLNESS

Lip print fullness shows how expressive you are verbally, and specifies your listening, writing, and social skills and talents. Fullness, or lack of it, also indicates your thoroughness, frugality, and analytical and mathematical skills.

- When your upper lip is the same fullness as your lower lip, you have excellent communication skills: listening, speaking, and writing.
- Whatever you know, you know it well enough to teach others.

Every time you make your lip print, decide on the fullness of the upper lip and read that information. Then do the same for your lower lip. Obviously, if the lip prints are the same fullness, you're done. But if the fullness is different, first read the information about the upper lip and then follow with the lower lip. Then check out the other combinations for additional information.

UPPER LIP FULL

You're an excellent listener and problem solver.

- People like to share their difficulties and issues with you.
- You're good at getting others to follow your vision.
- You'd make a good project manager or delegator.

LOWER LIP FULL

You're socially oriented and generous with others, sometimes to a fault. Children and pets adore you. You might like to be a nanny, day-care owner, animal trainer, or pet walker. You like to work with others and enjoy sharing what you know.

- You definitely like to talk!
- You have excellent verbal and written skills, and could be a writer, speaker, or entertainer.
- If you're not doing any of these things, your lip prints are suggesting you try putting some energy into one. You will be pleasantly surprised at how good you are!

UPPER AND LOWER LIP AVERAGE

Upper Lip Average

You have good verbal and written skills and are a good listener. You work well alone or with others.

- Whatever you do, you take pride in doing a good job.
- You're not a perfectionist.

Lower Lip Average

You easily learn new skills and are happy to share your knowledge with others. You're good with numbers and the bottom line without being obsessive.

- You take pride in doing whatever you do well.
- You are on time and do your part without much supervision.

UPPER LIP AND LOWER LIP THIN

Upper Lip Thin

You are picky! You can drive others crazy with your drive for perfection. But when a project needs someone who is well organized, detail oriented, and will do a job as perfectly as possible, you're the one to call.

- You are amazingly good at finding new, more efficient ways of doing things.
- Thinking outside the box is your specialty!
- You might want to be an entrepreneur, researcher, marketing specialist, makeup artist—even a Lipsologist.

Lower Lip Thin

You're very analytical and excellent with numbers or statistics—things that must be exact. A hard worker and frugal, you like to be productive and efficient.

- You can stick to a budget.
- You're logical and self-controlled.
- You might want to be an engineer, scientist, banker, history teacher, architect, financial planner, accountant, Realtor, CEO, carpenter, electrician, or contractor.

COMBINATION: UPPER LIP FULLER THAN LOWER LIP

Keep in mind that you're looking for the upper lip to be full in comparison to the lower lip, which can be average or thin. This combination says you're an excellent listener and problem solver, but don't like to listen for very long. You like people to get to the point. You don't like others telling you the same thing five different ways. You got it the first time! You often know more about others than they know about you.

- You want to help others make a plan and get on with it.
- You think things over and choose your words carefully.
- You could be a psychologist, doctor, lawyer, human resource specialist, consultant, nurse, coach, bartender, or hairdresser.

COMBINATION: UPPER LIP THINNER THAN LOWER LIP

You may not always listen as well as others would like you to. You're probably thinking about what you want to do or say, or you're distracted by new ideas. You can be so into your own thoughts that you don't listen at all. Though you may have been told something or requested to do something, you don't remember it because you're so distracted. Write things down: you need to be reminded of what needs to be done.

- It's important for you to make eye contact.
- The ability to concentrate on your own thoughts would make you an excellent scientist or inventor.

Fullness Story

I did a private reading for Lisa and later received this heartwarming testimonial.

> Jilly Eddy's lip reading changed my life. In my lip prints, she saw that I was at a crossroads, indecisive, and terrified. After twenty-five years living an adventurer's lifestyle, I needed a real job, but there were significant obstacles: I lacked a college degree, lived in a rural area, and didn't want to commute.
>
> "Tell me what you would love to do. What would be fulfilling? What would give you joy?" she prompted. "Think big."
>
> I was skeptical, but I confessed I really enjoyed writing, despite not having any formal writing experience.
>
> "Yes! Think about what being a successful writer might feel like, relax, and be open to receiving the goodness you deserve. Don't be afraid to say yes."
>
> Six weeks later, the editor of our local newspaper asked if I'd be interested in volunteering to write a quarterly column. I've just wrapped up my seventh year as executive editor of that same award-winning local newspaper. When Jilly Eddy's lips move, I listen.
>
> —Lisa Bryan, Executive Editor at *Key Peninsula News*

COMBINATION: UPPER LIP OVERREACHES LOWER

You tend to lovingly look out for others. It's not unusual for you to be responsible for a brood of children, siblings, or even chickens. Or perhaps you're always surrounded by a flock, whether it's animals or adults, to the point of neglecting your own needs.

- Sometimes the needs of others overshadow yours.
- If this is happening, you would be wise to take time for your own needs.
- You may have to speak up and let others know you would appreciate some help and/or a break.

COMBINATION: LOWER LIP OVERREACHES UPPER

You typically have lots of personal things going on and may have challenges others aren't aware of. You may be focused on a complicated project or taking a sabbatical. You may not have much time for doing things with others. Asking for help sometimes is a good idea.

- Having time to relax, by yourself, in your own space, is important and enjoyable for you.
- Keep in mind some people may not understand your choice to be alone, or not asking for help when you need it. Perhaps you can offer some explanation, without offering too many details.

EXTREME

MODERATE

SLIGHT

NO HUG PUCKER

RECESSED

STRESS LINES

LOWER LIP
MODERATE/
SLIGHT

HUG PUCKER

The Hug Pucker is located on the center inside edge of both the upper and lower lip. It has many shapes. Look carefully: You could see a thin or wide bump or mushroom peeking out, or an oblong shape like a little Vienna sausage. The Hug Pucker's name is associated with showing affection by hugging and puckering up to give kisses. The upper lip shapes come in various configurations: from extreme to not showing at all, to recessed in the body of the lip print. There can also be vertical white stress lines in the middle of the Hug Pucker that drain to the space between the upper and lower lip. Don't confuse these with the white lines that form the sides indicating a recessed Hug Pucker (see "Hug Pucker with Stress Lines," page 47). The lower lip has only one Hug Pucker shape, moderate to slight.

HUG PUCKER UPPER LIP

The Hug Pucker on the upper lip reveals information about the way you show affection, how much affection you want or need, and your way of interacting and communicating your feelings, actions, and expectations with loved ones.

Extreme

If you have an extreme Hug Pucker, you need a BIG HUG right now! You would appreciate extra support and affection from family and friends. Sometimes others aren't aware of what's happening in your life, but chances are they would be glad to help if they knew.

- You may need to ask for some hugs or assistance.
- Don't expect others to read your mind.
- It could also help to verbalize what's making you feel like you need a hug.

Moderate

You give wonderful teddy bear hugs. Upon meeting or departing, you're generous with your hugs and can be counted on to be the first to hug and kiss loved ones; usually you do this no matter where you are or the circumstances.

- In relationships, you want someone who likes to hold hands and hug, kiss, and cuddle.
- Find someone who enjoys being as physically affectionate as you are!

Slight

In public, you're not going to be the one who hugs first. You like hugs from family or close friends, but you're not likely to initiate the hug.

- In a relationship, you really don't like someone hanging on you in public.
- It's okay to let others know if you aren't a hugger.
- In private, it's a different story—you're more spontaneous when alone with your partner.

NO HUG PUCKER

When there is no Hug Pucker showing, there are two distinctly different meanings. Half of those who have no Hug Pucker will agree to the first interpretation, and half will agree with the second. Read both interpretations and decide which best describes you.

Interpretation #1:

- You're getting as many hugs and kisses as you want and need from your loved ones.
- You're good at letting others know if you want more affection.
- You like being able to just go ahead and cuddle, hold, or give hugs to your loved ones when you feel like it.

Interpretation #2:

Alternatively, you may not be getting enough hugs, kisses, or affection. This can be because you aren't interested, or you're busy and completely focused on your career, a project, taking care of family, or handling some kind of crisis.

- It might be beneficial for you to be more aware and work on being a little more spontaneous in showing affection, especially if you're in a relationship or have children.
- Those close to you will probably appreciate the extra effort and attention.

RECESSED

You can be moody—openly affectionate one minute and then want to be left alone the next. This can be confusing to others, who may wonder if you're mad at them. At times, you just need your own space, or you may want to be with only certain people.

- Communication is very important.
- Pay attention and figure out who would benefit from hearing from you (preferably in person).
- Though you may not be as openly affectionate or see someone as much as that person would like, it doesn't mean you don't love and appreciate all the other person does for you. Once they know, you'll be amazed at how things improve for everyone.

HUG PUCKER WITH STRESS LINES

If you have vertical white lines in your Hug Pucker, you're probably experiencing stress with your family or friends. Waiting for others to change or situations to resolve won't always work. Communication may be lacking.

- Disagreements, misunderstandings, or disappointments need to be resolved.
- Figure out what you can do differently to eliminate any conflict or confusion, starting with being kind and considerate of others' needs, while looking out for yourself, by taking control of what you can and getting help if you need it.
- It's important to let go and move forward, rather than stand still and be a victim.

HUG PUCKER ON LOWER LIP

The only Hug Pucker you'll find on the center inside edge of the lower lip is the moderate to slight one, and it looks like a thin or wide bump or mushroom peeking out or rising toward the upper lip. It has to do with how you treat yourself and how confident you are.

Moderate/Slight

You tend to give others recognition for their accomplishments, even pats on the shoulder, a hug or two, and kisses on their cheeks, but you're not always good at acknowledging yourself.

You may also be looking to others for approval or some positive comment.

- Your lip print is reminding you it doesn't matter what others know about your actions—what matters most is that you know.
- It's important for you to wrap yourself up in a big hug with a pat on the back in recognition for all you have accomplished.

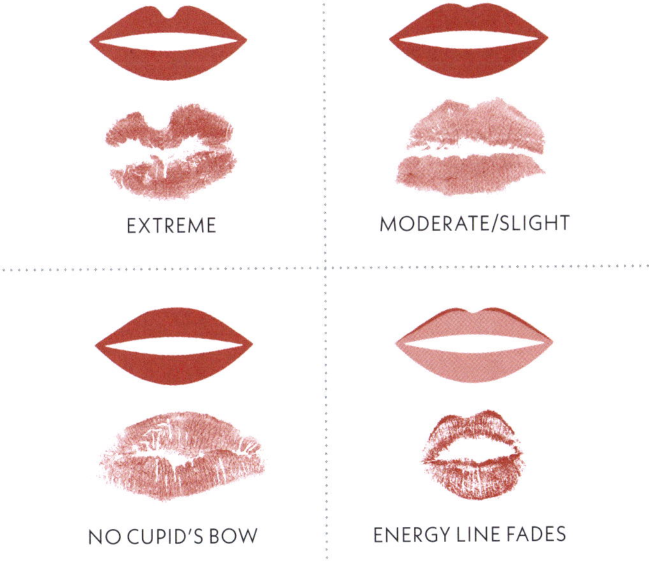

CUPID'S BOW

The inverted V-shaped indentation on the center outer edge of the upper lip is the Cupid's Bow shape we see when we look at a person's mouth. But not everyone has this shape, and even if you do, it doesn't always print that way. Cupid's Bow has many different configurations, revealing your temperament and interactions with others, and how you feel about your accomplishments. As your desires and goals change, so do your lip prints.

EXTREME

In the extreme V shape, the Cupid's Bow resembles the bow Cupid uses to shoot his love arrows. In Roman mythology, Cupid is the god of love, and his name means "to desire." This shape in the extreme signifies your strong desire to make a positive impression. You're attractive and charming and have a strong desire to increase the well-being of humanity. You look out for others, put a lot of energy into having good outcomes, but also like to receive appreciation and positive feedback. If you're not getting that feedback, you may benefit by asking for it and not waiting for others to be mind readers.

- Look closely and you'll notice that this shape also looks like a volcano crater, alerting others to stay on your good side—you have a temper!
- You may not show it often, but being pushed the wrong way for too long may result in an intense emotional outburst.
- You put a lot of energy into leaving a certain impression on others, perhaps by seeking to make a favorable impression at a job interview, or expressing yourself with extensive body piercing, elaborate tattoos, or wild outfits.

MODERATE/SLIGHT

You're usually even tempered, cooperative, and versatile, and an excellent negotiator with a keen ability to see both sides of a situation. Others' opinions moderately influence your physical appearance and actions. However, you can get caught between what you think others desire and what you desire. This is especially true when two or more of your lip prints, on the same paper, have the exact moderate to slight Cupid's Bow shape.

- When this happens, your lip prints are saying you'd be wise to look out for yourself first, in a kind and loving way.
- If appropriate, acknowledge that you understand the needs and desires of those you disappointed and explain that you really can't do what they want unless it feels right for you, too.
- If you do what others want you to do but don't really feel that it's best for you, it may be okay in the short term, but in the long run, it will not be good for anyone.

NO CUPID'S BOW

If you have no V-shaped indentation on the center of the outer edge of your upper lip print, this is called No Cupid's Bow. You don't like to be told what to do! You have your own style and way of doing things, and you primarily work to please yourself. You don't mind helping others, but people should not assume that you have time or are willing to help. They need to confirm first. If you are willing, you may also find it helpful to explain that you want only the project details and a timeline. You may even want this in writing. Then you'll want to be left alone to do the job. You work well alone, but can also be a good team player when it's necessary. You're very good at figuring out the best way to do things.

- You don't like to be micromanaged.
- You take good care of yourself.

- You're almost always even-tempered, courageous, and proud of your accomplishments.

ENERGY LINE FADES IN A CUPID'S BOW

Normally, an Energy Line on the outer edge of the upper lip extends almost all the way across the upper lip, revealing that others know you put a lot of energy into whatever you're doing. You work hard toward your goals and want to please others. But when the line fades in the area of the Cupid's Bow, the message is you're not feeling appreciated. Ask yourself: Are you feeling neglected at your job? In a relationship? When things are out of balance, you need to look to yourself to change and do things differently. If it's the job, ask for some tangible form of appreciation: more money, sincere thanks from your boss, or fewer hours. If it's at home, ask for more help or more quality time together—whatever will make you feel loved, seen, and appreciated.

- Figure out what you need and make it so.
- It's up to you to take responsibility and make positive changes, or to move on if necessary.
- When you do this successfully, the faded line on your lip print will fill in.

Cupid's Bow Story

My original definition of an extreme Cupid's Bow was based partly on the personality of a male fashion model I called Mr. GQ (see lip print below). He was also a construction worker, but he always looked ready to appear on a magazine cover. His clothes were cool, his hair was styled, and even his fingernails were manicured. He went a long way to pull off a positive impression. He also looks out for others, but he has a temper.

Sometime later, I was having dinner out with my sister and eight of her friends, and my sister asked me to read all their lip prints. I noticed Girl at the Bar watching us as she smoked cigarettes and drank beer. She sported multiple tattoos and pierced body parts, and was wearing a leather outfit with a tank top cut to her navel. She got her lipstick out, made a lip print, and thrust it toward me (see lip print below). "Hey, I want to do this, too." I took one look at that lip print and said, "Sure thing." She agreed with my assessment: She liked to make an impression, and did indeed have a temper. Girl at the Bar's lip print confirmed and expanded my definition, adding that everyone has their own way of defining a "positive impression."

MR. GQ

GIRL AT THE BAR

GOURMET LIP SPLIT

This V-shaped indentation is located on the inner edge of the center of the lower lip. Sometimes it looks like a small to large karate chop, a gentle curve, or all different sizes of funnels. Your Gourmet Lip Split (GLS) reveals your food preferences, sense of humor, and how romantic and sentimental you are.

EXTREME

You're not a cheap date! You enjoy delicious food and may be a gourmet cook or live with someone who is. At the very least, you know the best places to go. If someone wants to take you out for a special occasion, they'll need to know that you have champagne and caviar tastes. You're romantic and appreciate four-star restaurants, soft candlelight, nice music, and all the things that create a romantic mood. You're sentimental and good at remembering birthdays and special anniversaries. It's important for your special someone to remember special occasions, too. Overall, you're fun-loving and love the spotlight!

- You enjoy being pampered and living in luxury.
- You'd rather not have to work, but if you must, you need attractive surroundings with interesting people.
- You have a wonderful sense of humor and possess a delightful laugh that should be recorded so others can play it when you're not around.

MODERATE/SLIGHT

You enjoy food. You want to go to a nice restaurant, not a fast-food place. You prefer homemade meals over frozen dinners and enjoy having family and friends over for brunch or dinner parties.

- You're slightly romantic and sentimental.
- You have a good sense of humor and are fun to be with.

NO GOURMET LIP SPLIT

If you don't see a GLS, that usually means you're no stranger to peanut butter and fast food. Sometimes you're a pragmatic eater: hunger level + lack of time = whatever is at hand. However, this doesn't mean you're not a good cook and/or don't enjoy wonderful meals when the mood strikes or when something smells delicious. Maybe your gourmet leanings aren't being revealed currently because you're not feeling well, or you may have lots of other things on your mind.

- You have a good sense of humor, but sometimes others may not understand your special humor . . . People do think of you as funny, and they also may do an eye roll.
- Sometimes, out of nowhere, heartwarmingly, unexpectedly, you can surprise yourself and your sweetheart by mimicking your friends with Extreme Gourmet Lip Splits!
- In other words, you can be complicated!

> **NOTE:** Jilly says, "I know the 'No GLS' subcategory is spot on, because it totally describes me!"

DIFFERENT FOR MULTIPLE PRINTS

What if you made two lip prints at the same time, and one of them has a GLS and the other one does not? This usually means you're not a stranger to peanut butter and fast foods. However, it doesn't mean you aren't a good cook. It may be that your gourmet leanings are just not being revealed at the time.

- On the other hand, sometimes you prefer fast-food places.
- You may forget a birthday and not laugh at jokes.
- You may not be feeling well, or you may have lots of other things on your mind.
- In other words, you can also be complicated!

Gourmet Lip Split Story

At a graduation party, I read the lip prints of a young lady, and I told her that her lip prints said she enjoys food and could be a gourmet cook. She was delighted and hugged and thanked me. With a high five, she smiled and said, "Yes, right on! In fact, I'm going to culinary school next year!" She was relieved that her lip prints revealed she had made a good choice.

SPACING

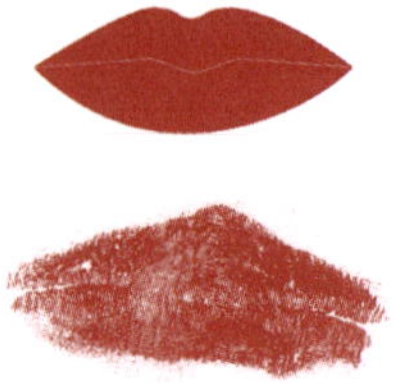

NO SPACING

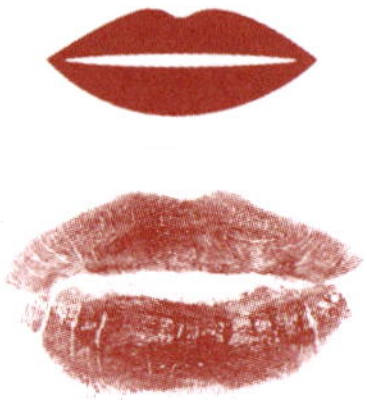

NARROW

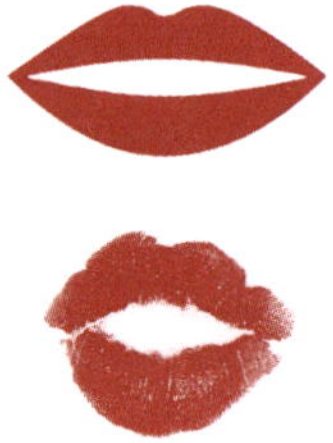

AVERAGE

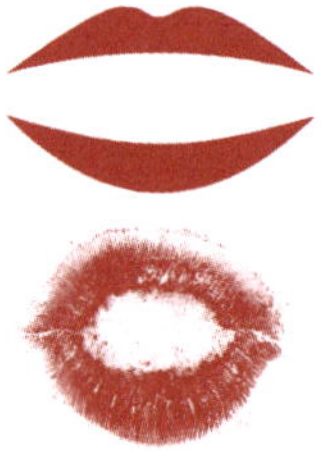

MODERATE

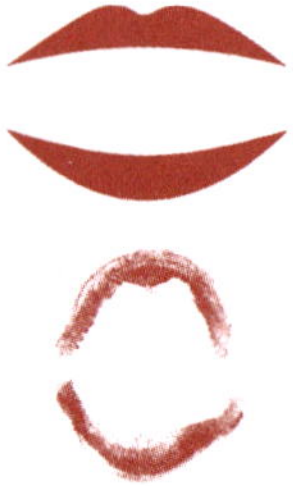

WIDE

SPACING

Spacing between the upper and lower lip indicates how open-minded or stubborn you are. Spacing also reveals your commitment to projects, how cautious or adventurous you are, and how honest and trustworthy you are. Two things to keep in mind when analyzing this feature of the lip print:

- The corners may be touching or open.
- Focus on how much space is between the inside edge of the upper and lower lip.

NO SPACING

If your lip prints are touching each other, or there is just a tiny bit of light showing between them, this indicates that you can be stubborn! You know what you want to do and how to do it. If you're going to be open to someone else's ideas or plans, that person had better have a really good story. These are nicknamed Missouri lip prints, as in the Show Me state.

- You might say, "Show me that your way is better than mine."
- You can also be a reserved observer and extremely cautious.
- If you don't want to do something, all the reasoning in the world can't change your mind.

NARROW

When there is a narrow opening, you'll listen to another's ideas, but if the gap is very narrow, you may just be pretending to listen. Although your mind may already be made up, you may give someone a chance to make their case.

- You're cautious, conservative, and not apt to take uncalculated risks.
- However, you may be persuaded to try new things.

AVERAGE

Even though you're not too wild and crazy, you do enjoy yourself.

- You tiptoe up and then jump in.
- You may not be the first to try new ideas, but you most certainly aren't the last.

MODERATE

You're open-minded and easygoing. You don't worry too much about things. You go along with others' plans and adjust where needed.

- You like to try new things and go to new places, though usually after researching them first.
- You like learning from others' experiences.

WIDE

You're open-minded and don't have preconceived ideas about people or situations. You like to hear all the information before you make a decision. You like to be free of limitations, boundaries, and restrictions. You look forward to new ideas, tastes, sights, and sounds. You leave the door open, and you want others to do the same. Rather than telling others what to do, you let others learn from their own mistakes.

- You want to be the first to experience and share your findings.
- Being extremely open-minded has its advantages and perils.
- Have fun but be smart.

SPACING IN MULTIPLE LIP PRINTS

When you make two or more lip prints at the same time, you should number them. This is especially important when reading lip prints with increasing or decreasing space, or if the space is the same. Regardless of where on the paper you place your lip prints, start your reading with the first one you made and then the next one. Starting with any other number may result in an incorrect reading.

To interpret spacing, we are concerned with the comparison of just two prints made by the same person at the same time. The spacing of three or more lip prints is complicated and covered in detail in the Lipsology Certification Course.

SPACE INCREASE

SPACING REDUCED

SPACE CONSISTENT

Two Prints: Space Increases

You're cautious at first, set in your ways, and weigh your options before venturing too far. You open up more as your comfort zone is satisfied. A little voice says, "That wasn't so bad, actually kind of fun. Let's try it again!" Your comfort level has to be satisfied with each move forward.

- If the space between the lips is just a little wider with each new print, you're an Incher, slowly moving toward your goals.
- If the space increases dramatically between the first and second lip print, you're very cautious at first, but once you reach your comfort level, you're gung ho!

Two Prints: Space Decreases

You're initially open-minded and ready and willing to try new things. But after you get your feet wet, you have a change of heart.

- You change your mind and pull back.
- You may even stop altogether.

Two Prints: Space Consistent

The space can be any width (narrow, average, etc.). The main criteria here is that the space between the inner edges of the upper and lower lip is the same, or at least almost identical, for two lip prints that are made at the same time. You're consistent and honest. People trust you. You walk your walk and talk your talk. If you say you're going to do something or be somewhere at a certain time, others can count on you.

- You have high moral standards.
- If you have an agreement with someone, your word is like a signature.
- If you don't want to try something, you have a reasonable explanation.

> **NOTE:** Keep in mind, if you don't have consistent spacing (that is, you have increasing or decreasing spacing) it doesn't mean you cannot be trusted! Your lip prints have their own meaning with no relationship to trustworthiness. See the preceding subcategories for information on what different spacing reveals.

CORNERS

UP AND CLOSED

DOWN AND CLOSED

UP AND OPEN

DOWN AND OPEN

CUT OFF AND CLOSED

CUT OFF AND OPEN

CLOSED LEFT SIDE,
OPEN RIGHT SIDE

CLOSED RIGHT SIDE,
OPEN LEFT SIDE.

CORNERS

Lip corners indicate how you deal with change. Corners also show optimism, pessimism, happiness, or sadness. You might be a pack rat, or a collector of things or information. Keep in mind, if your lip print corners are turned neither up nor down, you aren't overly happy or sad, respectively—or, at least, your print reveals neither. Consider yourself neutral.

UP AND CLOSED

You're happy-go-lucky, optimistic, and accustomed to things going your way.

- It takes a lot for you to make major changes.
- You're not looking for any major changes at this time.
- You don't like to be rushed when making a decision.

DOWN AND CLOSED

You're sad or upset at this time and could use a hug or a pat on the shoulder.

- You need to think positively.
- Even though you may not expect things to change quickly, your circumstances will improve.

UP AND OPEN

You're happy and optimistic most of the time and don't like to be bored—you'd rather be busy all the time. You're multitalented and do several things equally well.

- Change comes more easily for you when your lip prints aren't touching on the sides.
- Usually, the wider the opening at the corners, the more open you are to accepting major changes.

DOWN AND OPEN

You're not a happy camper. You need a hug or pat and some cheering up. Whatever made you sad or unhappy, you're ready for a change.

- Taking a different direction will be beneficial.
- Hopefully, you can see improvement.

CUT OFF AND CLOSED

You're extremely focused on taking care of business. You're like a horse with blinders on and may not be aware that others are concerned about you.

- You're trying hard to take care of many things—usually other people's wants and requests.
- Being so focused doesn't leave much time for any major changes at this time.
- Your lip prints want you to at least take some time in the near future to do something enjoyable and silly, just for the fun of it!

CUT OFF AND OPEN

You're doing your best to stay focused on taking care of business and going along with people and events.

- Although you don't usually rock the boat, you're wishing things were different.
- You're definitely ready for a change.
- The wider the opening at the corners of your lip print, the quicker you want the change and the more you're actively pursuing it.

CLOSED LEFT SIDE, OPEN RIGHT SIDE

You are holding on to the way things have been, yet you can adjust well to major changes that come along. Your lip prints also suggest you could be a pack rat or a collector of things and/or information. In either case, your interests are many and you have a tendency to take things in and not let go.

- Career-wise, you could be a historian, history teacher, researcher, or specialist in your field of interest.
- Your lips are saying: Live life to the fullest, yet please consider making room for expansion for other things.

NOTE: When you're a serious collector or pack rat and you love all your treasures, it's difficult to decide what to let go of . . . I know, I have over thirty thousand lip prints! Granted, they're not bulky, but I also have boxes full of wonderful lip-shaped things, and more in my house. Did I mention I also collect rocks? So enjoy your collection and take extra special care of it.

CLOSED RIGHT SIDE, OPEN LEFT SIDE

You may be holding on to the ways things have always been and want them to stay as they are. Similar to Closed Left Side, Open Right Side, this can also be the mark of a pack rat or collector of things and/or information. In either case, somehow things come in, and they don't go out!

- You tend to be sentimental and do not see the need to make changes at this time.
- Career-wise, you may enjoy being a dealer of antiques or books, or being a specialist in a field that interests you.
- Your lips are also saying: Enjoy your life and possessions, but please consider making space for other rewarding things.

CLOSED ENDS WITH INFO FUNNELS

INFO FUNNELS WITH ENERGY LINES

INFORMATION FUNNELS

These look like > or < and can be on one or both lip corners. It signifies that you need lots of information to make a decision, especially one that involves a major change. If the corners are touching just behind the > or <, you'll be very slow to make a decision.

You like to have a plan A and B, and maybe even a plan C. Look closely to see how the information funnels are touching.

- The more they're touching, the longer and harder it will be for you to make up your mind and take action.
- Be patient. If the Information Funnels are not touching, you'll make your choice more quickly.

INFORMATION FUNNELS WITH ENERGY LINES

These Information Funnels have dark lines, called Energy Lines, on their inside edges. These marks indicate that you have confidential information and you're very protective of it and are often visible in the lip prints of professionals such as psychologists, lawyers, or CPAs.

- Others share things with you that they might not share with anyone else.
- The information needs to be accurate because decisions or counsel are based on it.
- You may have to really study information (more so than others) so you totally understand it.

Corners Story

I met five-year-old Maddie at her grandmother's birthday party. She was very talkative, interested in playing with my lipsticks, and made lots of prints using different colors on different Kiss Cards. She then listened attentively as I told her that her lip print was open on the right and closed on the left. "You could be a collector or a pack rat," I said. "Do you know what that means?" She said no, so I explained the difference between a pack rat and a collector.

She thought for a minute and said, "I have lots of stuffed animals, mostly giraffes and monkeys, and I like to bring home shiny stones from the beach."

"Yes," I said, "that would make you a collector."

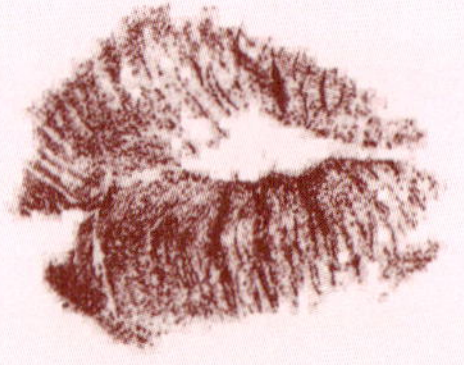

ZINGER

BLUNT ZINGER

SHARP ZINGER

ZINGERS

These are sharp or blunt protrusions coming out of the corners of lip prints and might be seen in all lip print shapes, though they are quite unexpected when found on round or oval-shaped lip prints (see Note on page 33). The marks can be extreme, like an ice pick, or very subtle, like a pencil eraser. If you see a sharp Zinger on your lip print, you can probably nail others to the wall with your words. You can be brutally honest or just mean, not necessarily intentionally. For any intensity of Zinger, it indicates you're well known for thoughtfully speaking your mind, and for using good judgment. You may be a lawyer or a doctor who says things others might not want to hear but must be said.

- You probably try to think before you speak.
- You're diplomatic when appropriate and more forceful when necessary.
- You quietly and constructively point out what needs to be said without offending anyone.

ANGEL WINGS

More feathery than Zingers, Angel Wings can be subtle or look like an amazing wing. If your lip prints show Angel Wings, you might already be known as an angel because you do kind, unexpected things for others, including children, adults, pets, even stray animals.

- You're a gentle soul always helpful to anyone in need.
- You comfort others and make them smile.
- You radiate love.

NOTE: Information Funnels with or without Energy Lines (see pages 68–69), Zingers (see page 71), and Angel Wings may show on only one or both corners and may be touching or not touching.

Angel Wing Story

In November 2004, I took a class on Chinese Face Reading at the Boeing Employees Parapsychology Club. At the end of the class, I mentioned that I collect and read people's lip prints. Everyone was quite interested to learn more. I gathered lip prints from several of the students and the teacher. The teacher's lip prints were quite unusual; they had a strange shape, especially on the left side, that I had never seen. I pointed to it and asked the teacher what she thought it could be or mean. She looked at it and with a big smile said, "It's my angel wing!"

A few weeks later in Portland, when I was entertaining at a holiday party, I saw a similar marking in a nine-year-old boy's lip prints. I called it an Angel Wing; his mother was amazed. She told me, "He is the sweetest, kindest soul I know. He's an angel, and that's what I've always called him!"

Thanks to special people like these who gave me hints about the meanings behind their marks, I came up with the perfect name: Angel Wings.

TEACHER'S LIP PRINT

features of the lip print:

uncommon marks

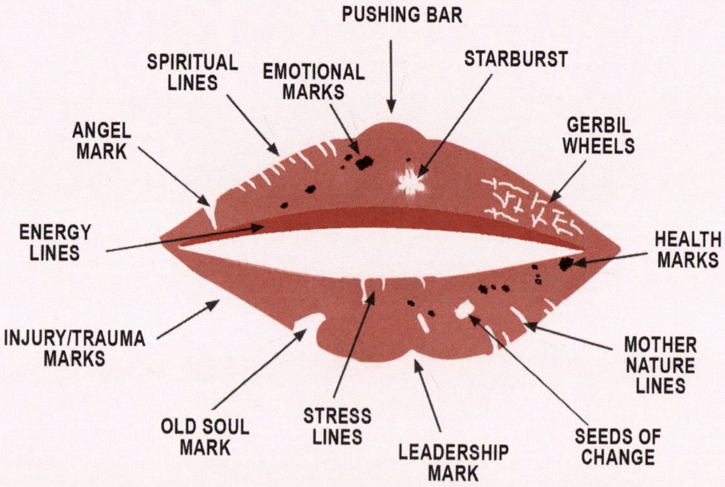

LIP MAP

uncommon marks

You may never see the following uncommon marks in your lip prints, but they appear more often than you might expect. Check them out:

- Starburst
- Mother Nature Lines
- Old Soul Mark
- Spiritual Lines
- Pushing Bar
- Leadership Mark
- Seeds of Change
- Gerbil Wheels
- Emotional Marks
- Health Marks
- Injury/Trauma Marks
- Energy Lines
- Stress Lines
- Angel Mark

Although the markings on the upper and lower lips can look similar, they may or may not have similar meanings. Both the appearance and location are very important. Read carefully and don't jump to conclusions.

Uncommon marks on your upper lip reflect your external world: how others perceive you, how you react to events and interact with others, and how you receive messages of spiritual guidance or connections.

Uncommon marks on your lower lip reflect your internal world, your private side. This can include career, health concerns, the strength of your intuition, and if you would benefit from getting outdoors more often.

Starburst Story

I had the honor of entertaining for the 2016 Maybelline/ *Entertainment Weekly* SAG Awards party at the Chateau Marmont in Los Angeles to toast the 2016 Screen Actors Guild award nominees. A large Maybelline sign was lit up behind a wall-to-wall counter with gorgeous hand mirrors engraved with *Lipsology*.

I had explained to Cara, my contact, that the Kiss Cards needed to accommodate the biggest possible lip print. I knew that people with large lip prints did things big. I told Cara, "There's a good possibility that the stars will have large lip prints. We'll need bigger cards." She increased the size of the Kiss Cards, allowing for just one lip print per card. With over four hundred guests, I didn't have a lot of time for each reading.

The DJ played loud music while movie stars, TV stars, and Maybelline executives partied and danced all around my station. I had to lean in close to each guest's ear so I could be heard. When one left the chair next to me, another sat down, eager to hear what their lip prints had to say about them.

"Whose prints did you read?" my excited family and friends wanted to know afterward.

"How can I know? I had my face buried in some wonderful-smelling hairdos. I don't know for sure whose prints I read."

One highlight was an actor whose lip prints were quite large, with what I call a "Starburst": a white dot or "burst of light." It's a very special marking on the upper lip. "It's the biggest Starburst I've ever seen," I told her. "It says you bring a brightness and positive energy wherever you go. The prints say that you're usually optimistic and upbeat and people are attracted to you and happy to see you. Whether you're with family, friends, or coworkers, you're very popular." I told her, "Maybe some of the people here tonight weren't going to come, but when they found out you were coming, they came just to have fun with you!" The last thing I told her was that the Starburst also showed she may just be the "favorite" of one of her relatives!

She grinned, stood up (all six feet of her), gave me a high five, and said, "Jilly, I'm everyone's favorite!" I'm pretty sure it was Hannah Waddingham, an actor in *Game of Thrones*.

It was a magical night of glamorous stars, music, and, can you imagine, Lipsology!

STARBURST

A white dot on your upper lip print is reflecting back to you a burst of light emerging like a new or well-known galaxy star! Your Starburst says you radiate a brightness and positive energy wherever you go, lighting up a room with your presence, personality, and smile.

- You're usually optimistic and upbeat.
- People are attracted to you and happy to see you; whether you're with your family, friends, coworkers, or even strangers, you are very popular.
- You may just be a favorite of one of your relatives! You know, like your grandma or grandpa?

MOTHER NATURE LINES

Vertical white lines on the outside edge of your lower lip indicate that you need to get outdoors for mental well-being. Regain your strength and energy by resting and relaxing, connecting with the beauty of nature, even hugging trees. Look at the beautiful sky, sit quietly, listen to the birds, and take time to smell (and touch!) the roses. Equally important, you need outdoor exercise, such as gardening, hiking, or getting a friend to walk with you to a nearby park to play catch. You'll benefit from the relaxation, the movement, fresh air, and the vitamin D absorption.

- You have athletic ability and may already excel in sports.
- If not, you would be wise to figure out what you might enjoy doing and try it; you may be pleasantly surprised at how good you are and how your outdoor activity balances your indoor activities.

NOTE: During my career, I entertained at a lot of high school grad-night parties. I knew if a student was an athlete even if they weren't wearing a letter jacket. A significant number of them had a Mother Nature mark on their lower lip.

OLD SOUL MARK

The Old Soul Mark is a little inverted V shape on the outer edge of the lower lip. It can have two meanings: a gift you give to others or a gift you receive. The message from your lip prints is that you can trust your intuition when it comes to making decisions.

The Old Soul Mark reveals that you're highly intuitive. There are things you know that you didn't learn in school or read in a book; you just know, and you're almost always right. You're here to share your gift of true wisdom with others. You may have a hard time explaining why what you say is true, but it just is, and others usually benefit from listening to your wisdom. Those who receive such information may not understand its value at the time, but it will make a major positive difference in the direction or path they take. Months or years later, they will say "Thank you!"

- Your lip prints want you to use your gift more, please.
- In addition, this mark says that it's important for you to listen to your intuition.
- The message here is to trust yourself.

SPIRITUAL LINES

These are vertical white lines on the outside edge of the upper lip, indicating you have a strong spiritual connection to the universe. Whatever you believe in, you believe strongly. It's a guiding, healing force and a comfort to you. The energy force coming down to you is similar to the rays of sunshine shining through clouds onto the ocean.

- Spiritual Lines might remind you of your strong connection.
- Sometimes it's a sign of affirmation.
- Either way, it's a lucky sign to have in your lip prints.

Spiritual Lines Story

Several years ago, I wrote to a well-known columnist to say that I enjoyed her articles and thanked her for her weekly valuable insights and words of wisdom. I explained what I do and asked her if I could have her lip prints for my collection, in return for a complimentary reading. She agreed and sent me her prints with a quick note that said, "Dear Jilly, Here you go—I'd be fascinated to hear what my lips say . . ." She was amazed with her reading, especially hearing the meaning of her lip prints' Spiritual Lines. She said, "You are so right. I am extremely spiritually oriented and have been since birth. Even when I was little, I never felt I was alone. I knew I was being watched over and protected by a committee of angels." She gave me permission to use her lip prints but asked that I not use her name, since this was a private side of her that most people did not know about.

PUSHING BAR
UPPER LIP

PUSHING BAR
LOWER LIP

PUSHING BAR

The Pushing Bar is located on the center (but not always dead center) outer edges of the upper or lower lip. On the upper lip, it looks like a little mushroom or sausage pushing out, indicating you have high goals and expectations for yourself and for others. They're aware of your determination and how successful you are. On the lower lip, the mark can be a narrow or wide bump pushing downward, revealing that you have high goals and expectations that others are not aware of. The harder you push, the more extreme the Pushing Bar becomes.

PUSHING BAR UPPER LIP

You push yourself, and others in your area of influence (significant others, spouse, employees, siblings, friends, etc.), to be the best you/they can be, pushing the bar to new heights. Once you reach your goal, you immediately raise the bar without acknowledging how well you or others did.

- You would be wise to take some time to bask in your glory and relax a little before starting work on another goal. Give yourself credit for a job well done.
- Take time to express appreciation to others. Who in your life would be happy to hear that, even though they aren't where you (or they) thought they'd be, you love them, are proud of them, and appreciate all they have done to get to where they are? Tell them in person if you can.
- Possibly you should listen to this message as well.

PUSHING BAR LOWER LIP

If you have this protrusion, you have very high private expectations for yourself that others are not aware of. You don't want others to know what you're aspiring to. In fact, others may think you just fell into good times and things come easily to you. The truth is, you have worked very hard to get to where you are, and you aren't done yet. Your lip print is reminding you to take the time to slow down, celebrate, and take a rest before automatically setting another private goal.

- If you find you're not where you thought you'd be by a certain time, be gentle with yourself.
- Give yourself a hug or pat on the back and be happy with what you've accomplished so far.
- When you reach a goal, remember to celebrate and rest.

LEADERSHIP MARK

The Leadership Mark is a slight curve or indentation in the center on the outer edge of your lower lip. It isn't usually large, sometimes hardly noticeable, but it speaks loudly about your ability and style of leadership, how you operate and achieve your goals, and some things you don't want others to know about you.

- Because of your position or job, you come across as tough, speak with authority, make hard decisions, stand up to others, and call the shots.
- Your interaction with others is about getting things done, not winning friends.
- The BIG secret: You have a soft side that you don't or can't reveal. In other words, you can be a sweetheart.

Leadership Story

I was the featured entertainment for a Pearl Friends fundraiser event to raise money for pancreatic cancer research. It was quite the gala. Approximately two hundred guests enjoyed an elegant evening of drinks, delicious food, and Lipsology.

Complete with Kiss Cards, lipsticks, pens, and mirrors on the tables, I talked about what I do, how I developed it, and why and how it's entertaining, educational, and fun.

Then I asked the guests to apply lipstick and kiss the Kiss Card two or more times. I assured them there's no right or wrong way to do it. I also asked them to number the order they made them and print their names (I don't like loose, unidentified lip prints).

I was on a stage being filmed so guests could easily see me on one of the two big, angled screens behind me.

I gave a short reading for three audience members. Their cards were projected onto the screens so people could understand the size, shape, and all the marks. The lip prints I read were from people who were well known by the audience members. After my reading, the person who made the prints stood so everyone could see who it was. The first two went well. The audience gave me a nice round of applause when I was correct.

I mentioned two things about the third person's lip prints, ending with a mark on their lower lip. I pointed to the center, outer edge, "Here's a slight indentation. This mark is most often seen on a woman's lip print. It reveals the person is operating in what I call a man's world. They must come across as tough, speak with authority, make hard decisions, stand up to others, and call the shots. They're more about getting things done than winning friends. They may be on a board of directors or the coach of an athletic team. But there is something not everyone knows about them.

"Do you all agree that what I say next, stays here?" With a show of hands, they all agreed.

"The secret is that this person has a softer side that they don't always show."

Imagine everyone's surprise when a five-foot-two, gorgeous blonde stood up and gave me a thumbs-up. "Spot on, Jilly! I'm an officer in the United States Marines!" The applause was thunderous. We got a standing ovation.

Another Leadership Story

I read for a lady who had a Leadership Mark on her lower lip. After I told her what it meant, she revealed she was, indeed, the coach of her son's basketball team. She added, "If you're going to coach a high school boys' basketball team, you have to be in their face and act like a man. You have to be tough, accurate, walk the walk, talk the talk, and speak with authority. Otherwise you won't be effective."

SEEDS OF CHANGE

Seeds of Change are white dots or small lines on the lower lip entirely surrounded by color; they look like a seed or grain. They indicate that you have an idea germinating; it can be in the incubation stage, or you may be improving and nurturing it but aren't finished. You might be trying to figure out what that idea is, or maybe you're not even aware of it yet. Either way, this mark is exciting to see and signifies that you are (or will be) doing something important that will be beneficial to yourself and many others.

- You're here to make a major difference helping others and you're on the right track.
- On the other hand, if you're not doing anything beneficial for others, this is a good time to figure out what you can do and DO IT!

GERBIL WHEELS
UPPER LIP

GERBIL WHEELS
LOWER LIP

GERBIL WHEELS

Gerbil Wheels are fine white lines scattered on the body of your upper and/or lower lip print. The name comes from gerbils running constantly on their wheels, which is much like the spinning of thoughts going on in your mind.

Gerbil Wheels on the upper lip have to do with your life at home, school, or work.

Gerbil Wheels on the bottom lip have to do with your heart and soul, what you want to do when you grow up, or something you want to change.

GERBIL WHEELS UPPER LIP

To help you work more effectively and without as much strain, your lip prints are suggesting you do this short exercise. In a quiet place where you will not be disturbed, bring some paper, a pen and a black marker. (You may want to use your computer, but I think it's more effective to write by hand, with no batteries or electricity—even work outside!) Make separate lists of things you want or need to do regarding home, school, or work. Start with the one that's spinning the most in your mind. Do this without censoring, just list "to dos" for today, tomorrow, and next week, no more than a month. Write freely until you can't write anymore. Then reorganize what you wrote, following these directions:

- Prioritize: List the most important things you want to accomplish first, second, etc.
- Get help: Pick two things someone can help you do. It's easier to see where you need help when it's written down.
- Delegate: Pick two things you're going to ask or tell someone else to do, then:
  - Write down *exactly* what you want them to do and give them your directions.
  - Tell them when you need it done. Let that person know you'll be giving them feedback before signing off because this gives you some control.
- Delete: Decide on two things nobody is going to do! Who cares if you don't do everything on your list? And when you consciously decide not to do something, let it go and don't beat yourself up later.
- Cross off completed tasks: Use black marker so you can no longer see what you wrote. This will stop you from looking at it and maybe even going back and making sure you're really finished.

Repeat these steps for your remaining categories. Good news: When you accept your lip print's message and successfully follow these steps, you'll have more energy and be more efficient. All of this gives you more time to rest and have fun!

GERBIL WHEELS LOWER LIP

When Gerbil Wheels are showing in your lower lip print, you're constantly going over what you want to do next or when you "grow up." To help you avoid having these lines turn into stress lines, your lip prints want you to find a quiet place where you won't be disturbed. Gather paper and a pen, and capture all the information running around in your brain, heart, and soul. If you could do anything you want, with no concern for cost, time, or what other people think, what would you love to do?

- Write freely, until you can't write anymore, with no censoring.
- When you've finished writing, put your notes away for a day, or up to a month. Waiting gives you breathing room so you can be open and ready for what you'll discover.
- When you're ready, read and reorganize your notes into baby steps toward doing what you're passionate about! Barbra Streisand once said on Bravo's *Inside the Actors Studio*, "At the moment of commitment, the universe conspires to assist you."
- Once your notes are rewritten, destroy the original writings.
- Let go, and trust that your choices will become clear, and that the universe will happily assist you!
- Expect answers. Be sure to pay attention to the affirmations that come your way.
- Believe dreams really do come true. I know because this is exactly what happened to help me bring Lipsology to the world. Thank you, universe.

EMOTIONAL MARKS

Dark, pepper-like dots on your upper lip are called Emotional Marks. There might be a few spots or one big dot. These marks are telling you that something or someone is irritating you. You'll need to figure out the valuable lessons learned from dealing with other people or events and how to move forward. You're emotionally holding something back that you'd like to express to someone else. The mental strain is diminishing, or temporarily obstructing your progress.

- Pay attention to what's bothering you and find a solution.
- Your lips will be soothed and smoothed!
- Amazingly, if none of the above makes sense, or seems appropriate to you, perhaps you're looking for someone or something to spice up your life? What fun . . .

HEALTH MARKS

Dark dots like black pepper or smudges scattered across your lower lip are called Health Marks. These dark dots indicate you need to pay attention to your health. It can be as simple as being dehydrated and needing to drink more water.

- You may be pregnant, and of course need to stay healthy for both of you.
- Maybe it's your thyroid, blood pressure, or hormones? Consult your doctor!
- If you're unaware of any reason your lip prints have dark dots, your lip prints are suggesting you would be wise to find out.

Health Marks Story

Barbara asked me to read her lip prints before a Mardi Gras gala. (I had read her lip prints about eight months earlier; see below left.) All dressed up, she looked fine, but her lip prints revealed that she wasn't fine. They told a disturbing story about her energy and health, showing a combination of Ghost Lips, Stress Lines, Health Marks, and Gale Marks (see below right).

"What's going on with you?" I asked. "Your lip prints indicate you're exhausted, stressed, and going through a difficult situation. Something's not right with your health and you need to do something about it."

She shook her head in amazement and said she hadn't been feeling well. "I'm very worried and anxious to find out what's going on. I had an MRI and an ultrasound, and my doctor is running blood tests. I'll get the results on Monday." I reminded her that the love of family and friends would help her through this difficult period.

She called later and said, "They discovered a blood clot in my leg! I'm on medication and feeling much better."

Barbara's lip print indicated no health concerns.

Barbara's lip print indicated heath concerns.

INJURY/TRAUMA MARKS

A missing part on the outer edge of your upper or lower lip print reflects an imbalance, injury, or trauma. The side of the body affected corresponds to the missing part of your lip print.

INJURY/TRAUMA MARKS UPPER LIP

A missing part of the upper lip indicates an imbalance, injury, or trauma above the waist. This could be your upper back, shoulder, elbow, neck, arm, or possibly something having to do with your head, such as headaches, earaches, etc.

INJURY/TRAUMA MARKS LOWER LIP

A missing part on the outer edge of your lower lip reflects an imbalance, injury, or trauma to the lower part (below the waist) of your body. This could be your lower back, hip, knee, ankle, foot, toe, etc. Regardless of which side of your body is hurting, the main thing is: Do something about it. Don't just suffer.

If you haven't already gone to your doctor, consider visiting a medical professional. Think beyond traditional medicine and explore chiropractic, acupuncture, Reiki, or other naturopathic and holistic treatments. Also, positive thinking and talking to your body can do wonders. When nothing seems to help, ask yourself if your pain could possibly be because you're avoiding dealing with emotional issues. In his book *Healing Back Pain*, John Sarno talks about how focusing on our bodily pain distracts us from what's really bothering us. Please consider reading it. The amazing thing is, once you figure out what's needed, do it and you'll no longer have pain. The missing part of your lip print will fill in.

- You may tend to put off doing anything until you can't stand it anymore. Or you might get frustrated when you're not getting better as fast as you'd like.
- Your lip prints recommend you try new things if the old ones aren't helping.

NOTE: You might say, "Yes, I have an injury or pain, but it's on the other side of my body." This probably means that you're overcompensating, and the non-injured side isn't happy.

DARK LINE ON UPPER OUTER EDGE

DARK LINE ON LOWER OUTER EDGE

DARK LINES ON UPPER AND LOWER OUTER EDGES

DARK LINE ON UPPER INNER EDGE

DARK LINE ON LOWER INNER EDGE

DARK LINES ON UPPER AND LOWER INNER EDGES

LIP PRINT WITHIN A LIP PRINT

ENERGY LINES

Energy Lines are dark lines on the outer and inner edges of the upper and lower lips. They can go from corner to corner or just part way. Energy Lines may also appear in the lip corners (see "Information Funnels with Energy Lines," page 69). Energy Lines indicate where and how strongly your energies are focused.

DARK LINE ON UPPER OUTER EDGE

You put lots of energy into whatever you're doing.

- This could be your career, a relationship, schoolwork, or maybe a special project.
- Others are aware of your plans and how hard you're working toward achieving your goals.

DARK LINE ON LOWER OUTER EDGE

Others aren't aware of the extreme amount of energy you're focusing on your personal matters.

- This could be a career change, caring for a loved one, writing a book, or a spiritual discovery.
- It's an endeavor you feel you must handle alone.
- Please consider, it's okay to ask for assistance or a little help. You may be surprised by who will help.

DARK LINES ON UPPER AND LOWER OUTER EDGES

These dark lines look as if you completely outlined the outer edge of both your upper and lower lips with marking pen or lip liner. I call them "Stretch Marks" because they remind me of a rubber band. If you see these marks in your lip print, you're busy doing things others are aware of and you're busy doing things others are not aware of. Your plate is full, and you're stretched to the max. When you see Stretch Marks in your lip prints, it can be helpful to do the following:

- Write the word "normally." Then say it slowly.
- Remember, not too fast. It helps to practice in front of a mirror, saying it very slowly, with conviction. "NOOOORMALLY, I would be glad to help you, but right now, my Lipsologist, Jilly Eddy, says I'm not allowed to take on another project."
- Notice I didn't ask you to say "no." First, you're not good at saying no, and second, people aren't used to hearing you say no.
- Saying "Normally, I would . . . ," gives you some breathing room.
- Don't let someone give you a hard time over this. We don't want that stretched-out rubber band to snap!
- So, take care of yourself and remember to start with, "Normally . . ."

DARK LINE ON UPPER INNER EDGE

This line indicates guarded emotions. If you have this mark on your lip print, you have a protective shield up and don't show your true emotions unless you're sure no one will misunderstand.

- Others have to prove themselves to you.
- Only after you really trust someone will you open up.

DARK LINE ON LOWER INNER EDGE

This line implies that you are protective of your feelings. Your feelings are easily hurt. You like to wait until you know someone well before getting close

- Try not to be too sensitive to others' comments or actions.
- Get all the facts and don't jump to conclusions before you decide what's going on with others.

DARK LINES ON UPPER AND LOWER INNER EDGES

A protective energy surrounds your emotions, indicating you can be extremely difficult to get close to. Others must prove themselves, but once they do, you're the best friend ever.

- You probably still have friendships you made long ago.
- These are Keepers, aka BFFs—people who reciprocate exceptional kindness and friendship.

LIP PRINT WITHIN A LIP PRINT

Energy lines can have another meaning. Look closely and see a "Lip Print within a Lip Print"—a unique and lucky sign that says you're almost always blessed with an extra boost of energy when you need it.

- The darker the lines, the stronger the energy.
- Be aware, however, that if this coloring fades or becomes mottled, it says you're misusing this gift and need a rest.

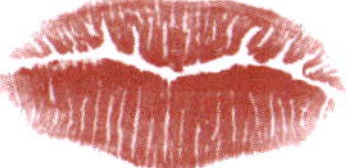

VERTICAL LINES ON THE UPPER LIP

VERTICAL LINES ON THE LOWER LIP

VERTICAL LINES ON UPPER AND LOWER LIP

GALE MARK

HORIZONTAL LINE ACROSS UPPER LIP

HORIZONTAL LINE ACROSS LOWER LIP

STRESS LINES

Stress Lines are white lines appearing in several configurations. They indicate drained energy and stress due to frustration, and difficult or disappointing situations. These lines may be vertical or horizontal; they may go all the way through your lip print or end partway, and they may be on the upper lip or the lower lip or both.

When you see stress lines in your lip prints, always be gentle with yourself and open to thinking about your situation in a different way. See this as an opportunity to listen to what your prints are telling you and take some baby steps toward positive changes. If you're reading for someone and you see Stress Lines in their lip prints, always be kind and thoughtful. Since these marks can indicate very sensitive issues, it's wise to assess the situation and make sure it's appropriate to discuss those issues with them. Say something comforting or ask if they need a hug. Pay attention to the individual's response and proceed accordingly.

VERTICAL LINES ON THE UPPER LIP

Vertical white lines start on the inside edge of the upper lip and end within the body of the lip. These markings reveal you're an outward worrier dealing with people or events you have limited control over. Since you may be unable to fix these things, figure out what you can do differently to feel less physically tired and emotionally drained.

- Look out for yourself in a kind and loving way.
- Stress-reducing suggestions:
  - Talk to someone you trust.
  - Make a plan for what you're going to do differently—and then do it!
  - Trust yourself. Let go of hesitation!
  - Don't try to fix everything.
- Making changes in a caring way, whether personal or professional, without worrying about everyone else, allows you to regain control and feel better and more energetic.

VERTICAL LINES ON THE LOWER LIP

These vertical white lines start on the inside edge of your lower lip and end within the body of the lip. These lines indicate you're an inner worrier. Others see you as carefree. The truth is, you privately rehash things that are bothering you, and this can be an energy drain.

- Stress Lines on your lower lip relate to your private life, where you have some control.
- Decide what you can do differently so you don't feel so stressed.
- Follow the stress-reducing tips discussed on the previous page, do your best, and go forward! You'll feel better and have more energy.

VERTICAL LINES ON UPPER AND LOWER LIP

These vertical white lines start on the inner edges of both the upper and lower lip. They reveal you're often totally stressed, and definitely the worrier in the group.

- Your friends and family are aware of this and love you anyway.
- Even though you fret over every little thing, you're endearingly protective and look out for others.
- Try the stress-reducing suggestions on the previous page.

GALE MARK

The Gale Mark is a white line that goes all the way through either the upper or lower lip. The lip print looks entirely split by a thin line or a wide gap, revealing you're living in a difficult situation and/or have experienced a loss or separation from a loved one.

- Regardless of where the Gale Mark is, your lip prints want to remind you that time, love, support of family and friends, and whatever you believe in are helping you weather your gale storm.
- And like a windstorm, this can cause havoc and destruction, but it doesn't last forever.
- When it's over you'll find renewed growth and strength, and the Gale Marks will fill in.

HORIZONTAL LINE ACROSS UPPER LIP

This line indicates that something or someone disappointed you, or that things just didn't work out the way you wanted.

- Your lip prints want you to ask yourself, "What did I learn?"
- What can you do differently so next time you don't feel this way?

HORIZONTAL LINE ACROSS LOWER LIP

This mark indicates that you might be disappointed with yourself. There is something you feel you didn't do exactly right or to the best of your ability. Or something you didn't do and wish you had.

- The message here is, "What did I learn?"
- Take this time to grow and not beat yourself up.

ANGEL MARK

The Angel Mark looks like a V located to the left or right of center, on the outside edge of your upper lip. Don't confuse this mark with the moderate to slight Cupid's Bow (see page 50). An Angel Mark indicates the presence of a guardian angel or guide on your shoulder. Usually there's just one mark, but sometimes there are multiple Angel Marks. Either way, it's a lucky mark to have! Its presence has several meanings. One is that someone is looking out for you. Sometimes this strong connection is to a loved one who is either living far away or has died. It may also be a guide or an angel who has adopted you. It's important to pay attention and be aware of their communications, whether you can see your angel(s) or not.

Anne Rice wrote, "Wherever and however they appear, angels offer consolation. They smile with infinite patience. They look lovingly on those of us whom they guard. Friends offering angel gifts are seeking to remind us that angels provide safety."[1]

1. "Anne Rice: The Angels Among Us," article in *Seattle Times, Parade Magazine,* December 20, 2009.

Your angels are helping to open doors and create positive opportunities for you.

- This mark also says that something may have happened to you that would make you wonder why you're still here. Your angel or guide provided you protection because your time wasn't up.
- Your job is to pay attention and take advantage of your good fortune.
- You still have important things to accomplish. The world is waiting!

Angel Mark Story

I read a lady's lip print who had an Angel Mark. She said, "You're right, I have this strong connection with my mom. She died several years ago, but she makes her presence known in the form of a ladybug. A month ago I had to fly and I hate flying. I was very nervous during takeoff until I noticed a ladybug on the seat next to me. That was Mom reminding me everything was going to be all right."

TOP ROW LEFT COLUMN	TOP ROW MIDDLE COLUMN	TOP ROW RIGHT COLUMN
MIDDLE ROW LEFT COLUMN	MIDDLE ROW MIDDLE COLUMN	MIDDLE ROW RIGHT COLUMN
BOTTOM ROW LEFT COLUMN	BOTTOM ROW MIDDLE COLUMN	BOTTOM ROW RIGHT COLUMN

POSITION OF PRINTS ON PAPER

The position of your lip prints on paper ties everything together. Just as each lip print has many things to say, so does its position on the paper. Imagine the paper divided into three columns and three rows to define nine zones.

Of course, lip prints don't always land in a specific zone. When this happens, you should read all the descriptions for the zones that your prints fall into.

- The sequence in which you made your prints is also important—it indicates what's most important to you and what path you're on at this time.
- Multiple prints in a column or row reinforce the focus of the position.

ZONES

Top Row, Left Column

Your thinking, planning, and dreaming include lots of memories and paths you have gone down. Are you ready for a change? Are you completely comfortable, or somehow stuck? Consider writing about your situation. Talking with family and friends can help you make good decisions.

Top Row, Center Column

You're doing a lot of dreaming, thinking, planning, and maybe even some soul-searching about what you're doing—or want to stop or start doing—right now.

Top Row, Right Column

Your dreams and thoughts are for the future. Thinking ahead and setting goals helps you achieve your desires.

Middle Row, Left Column

Maybe you're happy and don't want to leave your comfort zone, or you're tired of doing the same old thing but afraid of change, so you continue to stay with what you know. Whichever it is, positive or negative, your lip prints say you do have choices. You could choose to try something new. You might like it!

Middle Row, Center Column

You're living in the moment—the here and now—and dealing with whatever comes your way. What's most important for you to consider, learn from, and act upon today is reflected in the intricacies of your lip print.

Middle Row, Right Column

What will happen if you continue on the course you've set? By paying attention to your lip prints' messages, you can make wise decisions and continue successfully, or make adjustments where needed.

Bottom Row, Left Column

Your comfort level is tied in some way to your past. Whatever has worked for you before—and perhaps for a very long time—you continue to do. You're comfortable with your old possessions, and you may resent anyone trying to make you modernize.

Bottom Row, Center Column

Right here, right now, your creature comforts and material possessions are important to you. Decisions to add to or change anything in these areas may have your attention.

Bottom Row, Right Column

You are thinking about what you need to do in the future to ensure your comfort and maintain your possessions.

CONCLUSION

The spirit of reading lip prints—the art and science of Lipsology—is to provide a form of entertainment that sparks a twinkle in your eye and moves you to laugh out loud, blink back tears, or just get to know yourself, your friends, and your family a little better. It can surprise you with wonderful, unexpected experiences, provide amazing insights, and give affirmations that warm your heart and stimulate your imagination.

Lipsology provides meaningful and personal readings for you to think and talk about, as well as an opportunity to be playful. It can help bring people closer together—especially these days, when personal interaction seems more limited than ever.

With computers, the web, cell phones, and social media, we're spending more time looking at a screen rather than being with people. Even people walking down the street stare at their cell phones instead of speaking to others face to face. We're missing subtle communication provided by smiles, frowns, tone of voice, and body language.

Granted, technology helps us stay in touch. Especially when we were isolated during the COVID pandemic, technology made it possible for us to see and talk with each other and to send messages and pictures. It enabled some companies to stay in business and employees to keep their jobs. Though not ideal, technology helped some children with schooling. Studies show, however, that lack of direct human interaction can lead to depression.[2]

There's something warm and friendly about giving, receiving, and reading lip prints. As an ice breaker, lip readings can be thought-provoking and offer opportunities for both serious and playful conversations.

You never know what you might discover about yourself. Maybe you're going through changes, and your lip print reading indicates you're on the right path. You may need a break from a hectic life, and even though you know you're overextended and exhausted—maybe you even talked about that very thing yesterday—only after seeing your Ghost Lips (see page 23) do you finally get the message to slow down. A reading can even affirm something you've been thinking about doing and haven't even discussed with your closest friends . . . whatever it is, I hope you'll be happy to see it revealed in your lip prints, and that it will encourage you on your path to the life you dream of!

Lip prints can also be treasured for sentimental reasons, whether it be of a loved one, friend, or even yourself as you were at the time you made the prints. My dear mother collected handprints.

2. *The Connection Prescription: Using the Power of Social Interactions and the Deep Desire for Connectedness to Empower Health and Wellness*, Jessica Martino, Jennifer Pegg, Elizabeth Pegg Frates, American Journal of Lifestyle Medicine, Oct. 7, 2015, https://pmc.ncbi.nlm.nih.gov/articles/PMC6125010/.

Years after my mother passed away, my sister gave copies of some of those treasured prints to relatives and friends. Lip prints, similar to handprints, can be a source of joy as mementos of our loved ones.

Whether you're reading them or not, always thank people for giving you their lip prints. Lip prints reflect the soul! Thank you for learning about this amazing process. Hopefully you will practice and have fun with Lipsology throughout your life.

xoxo,
Jilly

GLOSSARY

Angel Mark A V shape on the left or right outer edge of the upper lip; shows that you have one or more guardian angels looking out for you.

Angel Wings Feathery, angel-like wings located on one or both corners of your lip print; indicate you do kind, unexpected things for others.

Certified Lipsologist One who has successfully completed Jilly Eddy's Lipsology certification program. For more information, please visit www.lipsology.com.

Cheerleader Your lip prints are a solid, dark color, revealing you have lots of energy and are good at getting others to buy into your ideas.

Color Intensity Dark or light lip prints reflect your outward and reserve energies. Just because the color looks dark on your lips doesn't mean your lip print will be dark.

Column One of three vertical positions on the paper where you made your lip prints: left, center, and right, representing past, present, and future, respectively.

Corners Whether the upper and lower lip prints touch or do not touch, or appear cut off on the sides, reflects your attitudes and how you deal with change, information, and decision-making.

Cupid's Bow A V-shaped volcano-like crater located on the upper lip's center outer edge reflects how you operate and achieve goals.

Emotional Marks Dark pepper-like spots scattered across your upper lip print indicate something is irritating you. You might also be looking to spice up your life.

Energy Lines Dark lines on the outer and inner edges of your lip prints indicate where and how strongly your energies are focused.

Fullness The plumpness of your upper and/or lower lip print, from thin to wide, reveals your communication skills, thoroughness, frugality, analytical ability, and mathematical skills.

Gale Mark A vertical white line or lines dissecting your upper or lower lip print signify you are going through a difficult situation, which could involve the loss of or separation from a loved one.

Gerbil Wheels Scattered white lines inside your upper and/or lower lip print reflect a lot of mental activity and a need to write things down.

Ghost Lips A light color on both your upper and lower lip print reveals you are extremely tired.

Godfather/Godmother Square- or rectangle-shape lip prints indicate you are well-grounded in your beliefs and firm in what you will and will not do.

Go-to Person A square- or rectangle-shaped lip print shows that you are solid and reliable; the one to go to for help solving problems.

Gourmet Lip Split A V-shaped indentation on the center inner edge of your lower lip print reflects your eating preferences, sense of humor, and how romantic and sentimental you are.

Health Marks Dark dots that look like black pepper or smudges scattered across your lower lip indicate you need to pay attention to health issues.

Hug Pucker An oblong protrusion that looks like a little hot dog or mushroom on the upper or lower inside edge of your lip print has to do with how you treat yourself, how confident you are, how you show affection, and how much affection you want or need.

Incher If the narrow space between your upper and lower lip increases only a little with each additional lip print, you probably make decisions slowly.

Information Funnel A V shape located on your lip print corners, revealing that you need lots of information to make decisions.

Injury/Trauma Mark Missing outer edge of either the upper or lower lips; indicates that part of your body needs attention. Upper lip concerns the upper body, and the lower lip concerns the lower body.

Juggler A medium-size lip print; indicates you are able to handle many projects successfully.

Keeper Dark lines on the upper and lower lip edges indicate you reciprocate exceptional kindness and friendship and become a lifelong friend.

Kiss Cards A custom-made paper or card where you and your guests put your lip prints; can be plain or fancy.

Leadership Mark A slight curve or indentation in the center on the outer edge of your lower lip. It isn't usually large, sometimes hardly noticeable, but it speaks loudly about your ability and style of leadership, and how you operate and achieve your goals. It also indicates that you don't want others to know you have a softer side in private.

Lip Print within a Lip Print A second lip print embedded in your main lip print is a very lucky sign that says you are almost always blessed with an extra boost of energy when needed.

Lipsologist One who practices Lipsology.

Lipsology The art and science of reading lip prints.

Missouri Lip Print If your lips are touching each other in your lip print, or there is just a tiny bit of light showing between them, you can be stubborn and need to be persuaded to try to new ideas.

Mother Nature Lines Vertical white lines on the outside edge of your lower lip print that end in the body of the lip indicate that you have athletic ability and it's important for you to get outdoors for your well-being.

Old Soul Mark An inverted V shape on the left or right outer edge of the lower lip reveals that you are very intuitive and have true wisdom to share with others.

Peacemaker You have round- or oval-shaped lip prints and like when things go smoothly and everyone is happy.

Position of Prints on Paper Placement of lip print(s) relative to three columns, three rows, and nine individual zones on the paper.

Pushing Bar A little sausage or mushroom on the center outer edge of the upper or lower lip indicates you set high goals for yourself.

Row One of three horizontal positions on the paper where you made your lip prints: top, middle, and bottom, representing your thinking and goal planning, daily activities, and your comfort levels with your possessions.

Seeds of Change White dots or small lines that resemble seeds and/or grains, located in the body of your lower lip. They indicate that you will do things that help lots of people in a positive way.

Shape The overall look of the outside perimeter of your lip print indicates how successful you are and in what ways.

Size The overall height and width of your lip print demonstrates how you tackle projects.

Spacing The gap between your upper and lower lips in a lip print indicates your open-mindedness, commitment to projects, stubbornness, and how adventurous you are.

Spiritual Lines Vertical white lines on the outside edge of your upper lip print that do not go through indicate you have a strong spiritual connection.

Stretch Marks Dark lines on the upper and lower outer edges of the lip prints that look like a rubber band indicate that your plate is very full. You are stretched to the max.

Starburst A white dot located in the upper lip signifies your positive, upbeat energy. Seeing you brings a smile to others' lips.

Stress Lines Vertical white lines that start on the lip prints' inner edges and may go all the way through. Stress lines can also appear as horizontal white lines across the upper and/or lower lips. Depending on their position, they indicate that you have drained energy and are dealing with stress, disappointment, and difficult situations.

Talent Scout If you have triangle-shaped lip prints, you have a gift for spotting talent in others. Your lip prints want you to share that gift often.

Zingers Sharp or blunt protrusions from the corners of your lips indicate you tend to speak your mind.

Zone One of nine positions on the paper where you made your lip prints.

ACKNOWLEDGMENTS

My sister Connie Swigart-Harris offered her enthusiasm and willingness to help in any way, including fact-checking, reviewing the manuscript, offering valuable suggestions, and regularly reminding me to stay on target. With her calm demeanor, my sister Junie Veith offered moral support, encouragement, and good suggestions.

Mr. Max, my beloved, extraordinary, fifteen-pound tuxedo cat, was my constant companion, napping on paperwork and always ready for a cuddle break, reminding me to stand and stretch or eat a meal.

Without Marcia Breece, this book would not have happened. She was patient, kind, funny, brilliant, and a taskmaster when it was called for. She guided me through this process with professionalism and grace while wearing many hats. She has my undying gratitude.

Kate Zimmermann's vision of "what a sweet little book this could be" touched my heart and soul. She offered the opportunity for Lipsology to be known and practiced worldwide! I thank her and her team for their help and patience.

Thanks to Jean M. Auel and Lisa Bryan for allowing me to use their lip print stories.

Most importantly, I want to thank my wife, Marsha Kremen, for her love and encouragement. She offered technical support as well as emotional support throughout this process.

ABOUT THE AUTHOR

Jilly Eddy is the founder of Lipsology, the unique art and science that uses an individual's lip prints to assess their personality characteristics, energy levels, and so much more. She is the author of *Lipsology: The Art and Science of Reading Lip Prints* and *Lipsology: The Art and Science of Reading Lip Prints Training Manual*, which is used only in conjunction with her certification programs.

For over thirty years, Jilly did private readings and entertained for corporate events and private parties, including product launches, trade shows, conferences, fundraisers, birthdays, weddings, retirement parties, and holiday parties. Some of her corporate clients included Avon, bareMinerals, Bourjois Paris, Clinique, Estée Lauder, Maybelline New York, L'Oréal, Yves Saint Laurent, Amazon, Costco Travel, Essex Property Trust, GGLO Architects, International Association of Women Police, Johnson & Johnson, Komo 4 TV, Macy's, Medicis Pharmaceutical, Microsoft, Nintendo, Nordstrom, Washington Athletic Club, the US Navy, and the US Air Force.

In 2007, Jilly gave well-received presentations at the International Behavioral Medical Biometrics Society Conferences in Budapest and Las Vegas. Another career highlight was entertaining at Maybelline and *Entertainment Weekly*'s celebration honoring the 2016 Screen Actors Guild Awards nominees at the Chateau Marmont in Los Angeles, CA.

Jilly described it as a magical experience—like being in a movie with stars dancing all around her as she read lip prints.

Jilly has been featured in many widely distributed publications, including *The Chicago Tribune*, *The Seattle Times*, *The National Post* (Toronto, Ontario), *Allure*, *Beauty Heaven* (Australia), *3rd Act Magazine*, *Grazia* (Germany), *Woman's Day*, *Woman's World*, *Marie Claire*, *Heal India Magazine* (New Delhi, India), *The Post and Courier* (Charleston, SC), and *Grand Rapids News*. She has presented her lip print reading system on television on *Cityline* with Tracy Moore (Citytv, Toronto, Ontario), *Breakfast Television* with Riaz Meghji (Citytv, Vancouver, BC), KOMO Northwest Cable News (Seattle, Washington), and *Crook & Chase* (Nashville, Tennessee). She has also been interviewed on numerous national and international radio shows and blogs.

Jilly retired in 2019 and says she will always enjoy giving and receiving lip prints and lip art, as well as reading lipstick kisses and hearing from others about their lip print adventures. Jilly and her wonderful wife, Marsha, live happily overlooking an idyllic tributary of Puget Sound with their extraordinary tuxedo cat, Mr. Max.

For more information about Jilly, Lipsology, and the certification program, please visit www.lipsology.com.

KISS CARD EXAMPLES

If you're planning a bridal shower, Valentine's Day party, or theme party, you might want to incorporate lip print reading as part of the entertainment. You'll need somewhere for your guests to put their lip prints, and you may want to add more pizzazz to your event with Kiss Cards. Here are some examples:

Lips & Libation

Let your lip prints talk

Kisses here:

Date ____________

Lip prints of ____

Apply lipstick, kiss this card 2 or more times, number the prints, write your name and date

What do your lip prints say?

Kisses here:

Lip prints of ______________________

Date __________

Apply lipstick, kiss this card 2 or more times, number the prints, write your name and date